Celebrating
St. Patrick's Day

BY M. J. YORK

Published by The Child's World®
1980 Lookout Drive • Mankato, MN 56003-1705
800-599-READ • www.childsworld.com

Photographs ©: Jodi Matthews/iStockphoto, cover, 1;
Shutterstock Images, 4–5; Patryk Kosmider/Shutterstock
Images, 6–7; Tim Broadbent Pictures/iStockphoto, 8–9;
Sanit Fuangnakhon/Shutterstock Images, 10; Brent
Hofacker/Shutterstock Images, 13, 14; iStockphoto,
16–17; Paul McKinnon/Shutterstock Images, 18–19;
Thomas Barrat/Shutterstock Images, 20–21

Design Element: Shutterstock Images

ISBN 9781503816558
LCCN 2016945625

Printed in the United States of America
PA02324

ABOUT THE AUTHOR

M. J. York is a writer and editor
from Minnesota. She enjoys spring
rains and planting her garden.

Contents

Happy St. Patrick's Day!

It is St. Patrick's Day! We celebrate Irish **culture**.

This **holiday** is March 17. We wear green.

Green

The color green makes us think of Ireland. There are green hills there.

A shamrock is green. It is a **symbol** of St. Patrick's Day.

Fun Foods

We eat green food.

We eat green cookies.

Corned beef is Irish. We eat it. We eat cabbage, too.

Parades

Many cities have parades. We hear fun songs.

Dancers **perform** Irish dances. They wear bright dresses.

People in Chicago
dye a river green!
How do you celebrate
St. Patrick's Day?

Green Flowers Craft

Dye your own green flowers for St. Patrick's Day!

Supplies:

vase or glass water

green food coloring white carnation flowers

Instructions:

1. Fill your vase or glass with water.

2. Add 20 to 30 drops of food coloring.

3. Place the flowers in the vase with the stems down in the water.

4. Wait at least one day. The flower petals will get greener the longer you wait.

Glossary

culture — (KUHL-chur) Culture is the ideas and traditions of a group of people. On St. Patrick's Day, we celebrate Ireland's culture.

dye — (DYE) To dye something is to change its color. On St. Patrick's Day, people in Chicago dye the Chicago River green.

holiday — (HAH-li-day) A holiday is a day when people celebrate a special occasion. St. Patrick's Day is a holiday.

perform — (pur-FORM) To perform is to entertain an audience or put on a show. Dancers perform a dance.

symbol — (SIM-buhl) A symbol is a design or thing that stands for something else. A shamrock is a symbol of St. Patrick's Day.

To Learn More

Books

Keogh, Josie. *St. Patrick's Day.*
New York, NY: PowerKids Press, 2013.

Lynette, Rachel. *Let's Throw a St. Patrick's Day Party.* New York, NY: PowerKids Press, 2012.

Web Sites

Visit our Web site for links about
St. Patrick's Day: **childsworld.com/links**

Note to Parents, Teachers, and Librarians: We routinely verify our Web links to make sure they are safe and active sites. So encourage your readers to check them out!

Index

24